Plant-Based Buddha Bowls Cookbook for Beginners

365-Day Easy, Gluten-Free, Oil-Free Recipes for Nutritionally Balanced, One-Bowl Vegan Meals

Sime Tam

Table of contents

Introduction

This Plant-Based Buddha Bowls Cookbook makes it easy to turn fresh, unprocessed ingredients into grain bowls, salads, pasta bowls and soups that fuel your body and spirit for complete holistic health. Each recipe perfectly balances of rich flavors, varied textures and healing ingredients, all comfortably blending together in a comfortable bowl. Every bite will make your taste buds dance happily! Not to mention that your body will feel light, fresh and energized.

Grab your bowl, your appetite, and this book, and get ready to eat! Forks and spoons are optional.

Chapter 1: What Are Buddha Bowls?

Buddha bowls are the latest trend among yogis, health bloggers and people who love to take photos of their food and post them on their social media sites. However, it's important to know that there's more to the Buddha bowl than just being a share-worthy social media post. Also known as the hippie bowl, sunshine bowl, macro bowl, and many other names, a Buddha bowl refers to a bowl packed with food mostly vegetables and grains, but can also include meat or chicken, drizzled with tasty sauce, overflowing with both flavor and color.

What Is a Buddha Bwl Made of?

Although there are no set and clear rules, experts say that a Buddha bowl is composed of:
- 25 percent whole grains
- 15 percent lean protein
- 35 percent vegetables
- 10 percent sauce
- 30 percent extra ingredients (egg, nuts, seeds, sprouts)

But again, there are no exact guidelines, and this one above can be adjusted according to your liking. For example, you can replace vegetables with fruits, or skip the sauce if you like. Basically, a Buddha bowl is composed of the layers enumerated below, starting from the bottom part of the bowl.

Whole Grains

Whole grains such as brown rice, barley, bulgur and quinoa are usually the first layer that you'd put on your Buddha bowl. Why go for whole grains? As you probably know, these are healthier than refined grains, and would make you stay full for a longer period. This is why, Buddha bowls are recommended for weight loss. Eating one or two bowls a day is usually enough to keep you full.

Some ideas for grains that you can include in your Buddha bowl:
- Barley
- Black beans
- Brown rice
- Chickpeas or garbanzo beans

- Farro
- Jasmine rice
- Kidney beans
- Lentils
- Lima beans
- Millet
- Oats
- Pinto beans
- Polenta/corn grits
- Red beans
- Short grain rice
- Teff
- Quinoa
- Wild rice

Vegetables

A Buddha bowl is a great way to repurpose cooked vegetables from last night's dinner! But of course, you can also use freshly cooked veggies. You can even use raw vegetables like lettuce and other leafy greens.

As what any Buddha bowl expert would tell you, it's a good idea to keep it as colorful as you can. This is not just for the purpose of making the bowl look nicer on Facebook or Instagram but also to make sure that you get nutrition-packed veggies in your meal.

Here's a list of the vegetables that you can use:

- Acorn
- Artichoke hearts
- Arugula
- Asparagus
- Baby corn
- Beets
- Broccoli
- Beets
- Brussels sprouts

- Butternut squash
- Cabbage
- Carrots
- Cauliflower
- Celery
- Corn
- Cucumber
- Eggplant
- Endive
- Fennel
- Green beans
- Kale
- Leeks
- Mushrooms (buttons, chanterelle, creminis, porcini, Portobello, shiitake, trumpet, white)
- Onions
- Parsnip
- Peas
- Peppers (green, orange, red or yellow bell peppers, fresno, jalapeno, poblano, pepperoncino)
- Potato
- Radishes
- Shallots
- Spaghetti squash
- Spinach
- Sprouts
- Sunchokes
- Swiss chard
- Tomato
- Turnip
- Watercress

- Water chestnuts
- Zucchini

Lean Protein Sources

Buddha bowls are also said to be packed with protein. This is why, you need to make sure that you have a layer of protein packed food. Meat, chicken and seafood are obvious choices. But if you're a vegan or vegetarian, don't worry. You can get your protein from tofu, garbanzo beans, nuts, seeds and other protein packed vegetables.

Dressing

The dressing depends on what your taste buds feel like getting a taste of. But of course, you need to think beyond the usual commercial ranch or Caesar dressing. You would be much better off making your own vinaigrette or any other sauce that incorporates healthy and flavorful ingredients. You'll be happy to know that aside from the bowls themselves, there's a section in the recipe chapter that's dedicated to making dressings and sauces.

Nuts and Seeds

These are usually added at the topmost layer. Sprinkling a little bit of sesame seeds, chia seeds, sunflower seeds or chopped almonds does not only add more nutrients to the bowl but also more flavor and texture. These make the dish even more interesting and exciting. Kitchen experts recommend toasting the seeds in a skillet to add more intense flavor.

Consider including this in your Buddha bowl ensemble:

- Almonds
- Brazil Nuts
- Cashews
- Hazelnuts
- Macadamia Nuts
- Pecans
- Pistachios
- Walnuts

Bonus Ingredients

It's up to you what your "bonus ingredient" is. Most of the time, it can be a slice of mango or banana, or hard-boiled egg. There are no strict rules, but you just have to keep it healthy and wholesome.

Let's get to know more about the Buddha bowls and their benefits in the next chapter.

Chapter 2: Benefits of Buddha Bowls

Buddha bowls have plenty health benefits that you would want to take advantage of. But of course, you need to prepare your Buddha bowl the right way—choose lean protein, pack it with veggies and so on. We'll discuss the preparation tips in detail in the next chapter. But for now, let's get to know more about what these colorful bowls can do for you:

Benefit # 1 – Weight Loss

One of the most popular benefits of Buddha bowls is weight loss. In fact, if you're going to ask people why they're eating Buddha bowls, many of them will tell you it's because they want to lose weight.

Now the question is, does this actually work? Are Buddha bowls effective in helping people shed unwanted pounds? The answer is a straight yes.

It helps you lose weight through several ways:

- The whole grains help you keep fuller for a longer time, reducing sugar cravings and unnecessary snacking.
- Lean protein sources and other ingredients commonly used in Buddha bowls are low in calories and fat, so there's less for the body to burn.
- Even so, the Buddha bowl is packed with nutrients and energy-giving substances that make a person more energetic. With more energy, you can exercise more. And this leads to weight loss.

Benefit # 2 – Stronger Immune System

A major component of Buddha bowls is the vegetables. As you know, vegetables are packed with nutrients that support the immune system. Vitamin C, for example, strengthens the body's immune resistance, protecting it from bacteria, viruses and other harmful invaders more efficiently.

This is why, most people who eat Buddha bowls take note that they now suffer from fewer episodes of common cold, flu, cough, and other minor ailments.

Benefit # 3 – Increased Energy Levels

Most of the ingredients that you'll find in the Buddha bowls can help power up the body and supply more energy. If you make a habit to eat this type of meal on a daily basis, you will notice that you will feel more and more energetic.

You'll notice that you won't easily get tired even after a hard day's work. And that you'll still have plenty left to enjoy other things that you love to do at the end of the day. No more sluggishness and lethargy to complain about.

Benefit # 4 – Lower Risk of Major Ailments

It's not just the minor ailments that can be averted with the help of Buddha bowls. Buddha bowls are packed with vitamins, minerals and antioxidants that can help protect the body against serious ailments.

Not to mention, these are also low in sugar and fat, and do not contain any harmful additives commonly found in fast food and processed food products.

Many of its proponents believe that Buddha bowls can help reduce the following ailments:

- Heart disease
- High blood pressure
- High cholesterol
- Diabetes
- Arthritis
- Stroke
- Certain types of cancer

Although studies have yet to be conducted on the positive effect of Buddha bowls on reducing the risk of these diseases, it's important to realize that it has already been established in scientific research that the components of the Buddha bowls, specifically the vegetables, whole grain, nuts and seeds can effectively protect against these diseases.

Benefit # 5 – Improved Mental Health

Nuts and seeds are an important part of the Buddha bowl. And do you know what its top benefit is? Better brain health.

These foods contain omega 3 fatty acids such as docosahexaenoic acid (DHA) which is one of the major structural components of the brain. DHA is necessary for proper brain function and maintenance of brain health.

Aside from this, there have been reports pointing out that DHA can help slow down the progression of Alzheimer's disease and other mental problems.

Benefit # 6 – Better Digestion

Since a Buddha bowl is packed with whole grains, it means that it has lots of fiber. What does a lot of fiber mean? Better digestion!

Those who are suffering from digestion problems like bloating, gas, and irregular bowel movements have found relief after they've made Buddha bowls their daily diet.

Benefit # 7 – Clearer Skin

And because there are plenty vegetables (and thus, antioxidants) in a Buddha bowl, some say that this type of diet can also give you clearer and younger skin. As you probably know, antioxidants are powerful substances that fight off the free radical damage in the cells of the body.

Free radicals harm the body in several ways. These are also the ones that cause premature aging, making people look older than they are supposed to. Fortunately, their harmful side effects can be neutralized with healthy diets like Buddha bowls.

Chapter 3: Tips

To make sure that you're able to enjoy all the wonderful health benefits of the Buddha bowl, you must prepare it the right way.

Below, you'll find some tips on how to make Buddha bowls that are healthy and delicious, and at the same time, tips to help you save time and effort:

Tip # 1 – Use Organic Vegetables

There are many benefits to using organic vegetables. For one, organic veggies have been proven to have more nutrients and antioxidants. Since these are raised without the use of pesticides, you will not be exposed to harmful chemicals. People who have allergies to certain substances or preservatives also benefit from eating organic vegetables.

Tip # 2 – Go for Lean Protein Sources

If you'd like to lose weight or improve health, you'd want to go for lean proteins sources such as chicken breast, and lean cuts of beef and lamb. This means fewer fats to burn, and lower levels of cholesterol. As you probably know, high levels of cholesterol can be a precursor to heart disease and other serious ailments. Make sure that you only consume grass feed beef and lamb, and free-range eggs.

Tip # 3 – Use Healthy Cooking Methods

Instead of frying your meat or boiling your vegetables, it would be better to use healthy cooking methods such as stir frying (using only smaller amount of fat), grilling, baking and steaming. These cooking methods not only result in better tasting food but also in the preservation of nutrients. Steamed vegetables for example contain more vitamins and minerals than boiled veggies.

Tip # 4 – Watch The Portions

One of the purposes of serving the meal in a bowl is so that you can watch your portions. But if eat two to three bowls in one sitting, that defeats the purpose. Also, you need to watch the portions of the ingredients that you put in the bowl, considering the percentages provided in Chapter 1. This is important so you can enjoy the health benefits of the Buddha bowl without going overboard.

Tip # 5 – Make Your Own Sauce or Dressing

As mentioned earlier, it's not a good idea to buy commercial sauces and dressings. The ones you find bottled in the groceries are usually loaded with calories, fats, sugar and sodium. You'd be better making your own healthy sauces and dressings. Even if you keep the ingredients healthy, but you drizzle sugary or fat-laden dressing all over it, you can't expect to lose weight or improve your health.

Tip # 6 – Add More Flavor Using Herbs and Spices

Herbs and spices are a great (and healthy) way to add more flavor to your Buddha bowl. There are plenty that you can use and these include: basil, cardamom, rosemary, tarragon, oregano, pepper, chili powder, garlic powder, onion powder and so on.

Tip # 7 – Buy Pre-Chopped Vegetables

This time will help you save time, which is probably one of the reasons why you want to make Buddha bowls. You want to eat healthy and delicious meals without having to spend too much time inside the kitchen. Buying vegetables that have already been pre-chopped will save you a great deal of time and effort. Just double check to make sure that the pre-sliced vegetables are organic and fresh.

Tip # 8 – Use The Blender

Using a blender is another efficient way to cut down the preparation time. Instead of chopping and slicing the ingredients particularly for the sauce or dressing, you can use a blender or a food processor to speed things up.

Tip # 9 – Cook Ingredients in Batches

If you want to do your cooking in just one batch, you can cook the ingredients in big batches and then just store them in the freezer until you're ready to prepare your Buddha bowl. For example, you can make ahead your broccoli by chopping them into florets, steaming them and then freezing them until you're ready to eat. You can simply reheat the broccoli that you will use for your Buddha bowl for that meal.

Tip # 10 – Don't Forget to Exercise

It's important for people to realize that diet is just one part of a healthy lifestyle. The other part is exercise. Even if you eat a healthy diet rich in vegetables, fruits, whole grains and other nutritious foods, if you live a sedentary lifestyle and sit on the couch all day long, you can still end up suffering from health problems.

Be sure to get regular exercise as well. At least 30 minutes of moderate intensity aerobic exercises is good for keeping the blood circulating and the heart pumping.

So that's it! Now that you know what Buddha bowls are, what these bowls can do for your health, and how to prepare them the right way, let's go to the exciting part—making the Buddha bowls!

Chapter 4: 10 Basic Sauces and Dressings for Buddha Bowls

Avocado & Garlic Cream Dressing

Preparation Time: 5 minutes

Cooking Time: 0 minute

Servings: 2

Ingredients:

- 1 ripe avocado
- 3 cloves garlic
- 2 tablespoons olive oil
- ¼ cup fresh cilantro
- 2 teaspoons lime juice

Method:

1. Mix all the ingredients in a bowl.
2. Transfer to a blender.
3. Blend until smooth.
4. Pour over your Buddha bowl before serving.

Nutritional Value:

- Calories 166
- Total Fat 16.8g
- Saturated Fat 3.1g
- Cholesterol 0mg
- Sodium 4mg
- Total Carbohydrate 5.1g
- Dietary Fiber 3.5g
- Total Sugars 0.3g
- Protein 1.1g
- Potassium 258mg

Cilantro Tahini Dressing

Preparation Time: 10 minutes
Cooking Time: 20 minutes
Servings: 4
Ingredients:

- ½ cup tahini
- 1 cup cilantro
- 1 tablespoon lemon juice
- 2 tablespoons water
- 1 clove garlic, minced
- ½ teaspoon salt

Method:

1. Blend all the ingredients in a food processor.
2. Coat the top layer of your Buddha bowl with this mixture.

Nutritional Value:

- Calories 181
- Total Fat 16.2g
- Saturated Fat 2.3g
- Cholesterol 0mg
- Sodium 328mg
- Total Carbohydrate 6.8g
- Dietary Fiber 2.9g
- Total Sugars 0.3g
- Protein 5.3g
- Potassium 153m

Cashew & Bell Pepper Sauce

Preparation Time: 10 minutes
Cooking Time: 0 minute
Servings: 2
Ingredients:

- ½ red bell pepper, seeded and chopped
- ¼ cup raw cashews
- 1 clove garlic
- 4 tablespoons sweet chili sauce

Method:

1. Put all the ingredients in a food processor.
2. Pulse until smooth.
3. Serve with your Buddha bowl.

Nutritional Value:

- Calories 170
- Total Fat 8g
- Saturated Fat 1.6g
- Cholesterol 0mg
- Sodium 244mg
- Total Carbohydrate 20.4g
- Dietary Fiber 0.9g
- Total Sugars 14.4g
- Protein 3g
- Potassium 159mg

Lemon & Herb Sauce

Preparation Time: 10 minutes

Cooking Time: 0 minute

Servings: 8

Ingredients:

- 1 ½ cups cashew milk
- 2 teaspoons apple cider vinegar
- 6 tablespoons lemon juice
- ¾ cup almonds
- 1 clove garlic
- ¼ cup parsley, chopped
- ¼ cup cilantro, chopped
- ¼ cup chives, chopped
- Salt to taste

Method:

1. Add all the ingredients in a food processor.
2. Pulse until well combined.
3. Serve with your Buddha bowl.

Nutritional Value:

- Calories 113
- Total Fat 9.2g
- Saturated Fat 0.9g
- Cholesterol 0mg
- Sodium 78mg
- Total Carbohydrate 5g
- Dietary Fiber 2.6g
- Total Sugars 1.4g
- Protein 4.2g
- Potassium 200mg

Lemon Garlic Sauce

Preparation Time: 5 minutes
Cooking Time: 0 minute
Servings: 4
Ingredients:

- ½ cup water
- ½ cup olive oil
- 1 tablespoon lemon juice
- ¼ teaspoon garlic powder
- 1 cup firm tofu, chopped
- ¼ cup apple cider vinegar
- 2 tablespoons soy sauce
- ¼ teaspoon dried basil

Method:

1. Add all the ingredients in a blender.
2. Pulse until smooth.
3. Use as sauce for your Buddha bowl.

Nutritional Value:

- Calories 269
- Total Fat 27.9g
- Saturated Fat 4.2g
- Cholesterol 0mg
- Sodium 460mg
- Total Carbohydrate 2g
- Dietary Fiber
- Total Sugars 0.7g
- Protein 5.7g
- Potassium 128mg

Miso Sauce

Preparation Time: 5 minutes
Cooking Time: 0 minute
Servings: 2
Ingredients:

- 1 tablespoon miso paste
- 1 clove garlic, crushed and minced
- 3 tablespoons tahini
- 2 tablespoons water
- 1 teaspoon freshly squeezed lemon juice
- 1 teaspoon orange zest
- 1 tablespoon parsley, chopped

Method:

1. Combine all the ingredients using a blender.
2. Drizzle over your Buddha bowl.

Nutritional Value:

- Calories 155
- Total Fat 12.7g
- Saturated Fat 1.8g
- Cholesterol 0mg
- Sodium 348mg
- Total Carbohydrate 8g
- Dietary Fiber 2.8g
- Total Sugars 0.7g
- Protein 5g
- Potassium 133mg

Red Pepper Tahini

Preparation Time: 5 minutes

Cooking Time: 0 minute

Servings: 4

Ingredients:

- 3 cloves garlic
- 3 roasted red peppers
- ¼ cup olive oil
- 4 tablespoons lemon juice
- 2 tablespoons tahini
- Salt to taste

Method:

1. Add the garlic, red peppers, olive oil, lemon juice, tahini and salt in a blender.
2. Pulse until smooth.
3. Drizzle over your Buddha bowl.

Nutritional Value:

- Calories 174
- Total Fat 16.9g
- Saturated Fat 2.5g
- Cholesterol 0mg
- Sodium 181mg
- Total Carbohydrate 6g
- Dietary Fiber 1.5g
- Total Sugars 2.8g
- Protein 2g
- Potassium 150mg

Peanut Butter Sauce

Preparation Time: 5 minutes

Cooking Time: 0 minute

Serving: 1

Ingredients:

- 2 tablespoons peanut butter
- 1/8 cup soy milk
- Salt to taste

Method:

1. Mix all the ingredients.
2. Serve with your Buddha bowl.

Nutritional Value:

- Calories 68
- Total Fat 5.6 g
- Saturated Fat 1.2 g
- Cholesterol 0 mg
- Sodium 105 mg
- Total Carbohydrates 2.7 g
- Dietary Fiber 0.7 g
- Total Sugars 1.4 g
- Protein 3 g
- Potassium 81 mg

Teriyaki Sauce

Preparation Time: 5 minutes
Cooking Time: 0 minute
Servings: 2
Ingredients:

- ½ cup mango, cubed
- 1 clove garlic
- ¼ cup coconut amino
- 2 tablespoons raw honey
- 3 tablespoons sesame oil
- 1 tablespoon lime juice

Method:

1. Add the mango, garlic, coconut amino, honey and sesame oil in a blender.
2. Pulse until smooth.
3. Drizzle on the top layer of your Buddha bowl.

Nutritional Value:

- Calories 146
- Total Fat 10.3g
- Saturated Fat 1.5g
- Cholesterol 0mg
- Sodium 12mg
- Total Carbohydrate 14g
- Dietary Fiber 0.4g
- Total Sugars 11.5g
- Protein 0.3g
- Potassium 43mg

Savory Mayo Dressing

Preparation Time: 5 minutes

Cooking Time: 0 minute

Servings: 2

Ingredients:

- ¼ cup low fat mayonnaise
- 2 tablespoons water
- 3 cloves garlic, minced
- Garlic salt and pepper to taste
- Pinch of dried basil

Method:

1. Mix all the ingredients in a bowl.
2. Serve with your Buddha bowl.

Nutritional Value:

- Calories 107
- Total Fat 10g
- Saturated Fat 1g
- Cholesterol 10mg
- Sodium 281mg
- Total Carbohydrate 3.5g
- Dietary Fiber 0.1g
- Total Sugars 0.1g
- Protein 0.3g
- Potassium 18mg

Chapter 5: Breakfast Bowls

Granola Smoothie In A Bowl

Preparation Time: 10 minutes

Cooking Time: 0 minute

Servings: 2

Ingredients:

- 1 cup almond milk
- 4 cups mixed berries
- 1 banana
- 3 tablespoons granola, divided
- 1 cup strawberries, chopped

Method:

1. Blend the milk, berries and banana in the blender until smooth.
2. Add 2 tablespoons granola.
3. Pulse for a few more seconds.
4. Pour the mixture into bowls.
5. Top with the remaining granola and strawberries.

Nutritional Value:

- Calories 269
- Total Fat 17.8g
- Saturated Fat 13.2g
- Cholesterol 0mg
- Sodium 13mg
- Total Carbohydrate 35.9g
- Dietary Fiber 8.8g
- Total Sugars 19.7g
- Protein 4.6g
- Potassium 560mg

Overloaded Breakfast Bowl

Preparation Time: 20 minutes

Cooking Time: 45 minutes

Servings: 4

Ingredients:

- 1 zucchini, sliced into rounds
- 4 cups sweet potatoes, diced
- 2 bell peppers, sliced
- 6 teaspoons olive oil, divided
- Salt and pepper to taste
- 2 cups tomatoes, chopped
- 1 onion, chopped
- 2 cloves garlic, minced
- 8 ounces Portobello mushrooms, chopped
- 2 teaspoons dried rosemary
- ½ teaspoon dried thyme
- 12 ounces lean ground turkey
- 8 cups baby spinach
- ¾ cup roasted pistachios
- 4 hard-boiled eggs
- Hot sauce

Method:

1. Preheat your oven to 425 degrees F.
2. Toss the zucchini, sweet potatoes and bell peppers in half of the olive oil, salt and pepper.
3. Transfer to a baking pan.
4. Bake for 30 minutes.
5. While waiting, mix the tomatoes with a little bit of olive oil.
6. Season with the salt and then set aside.
7. In a skillet over medium low heat, pour in about a teaspoon of oil.
8. Cook the onions for 3 minutes.
9. Add the garlic and mushrooms.
10. Cook for 1 minute.
11. Season with the herbs.
12. Add the ground turkey.
13. Cook until brown and then transfer to a plate. Set aside.
14. Remove the sweet potatoes from the oven. Set aside.
15. Add the remaining oil to the pan.

16. Cook the spinach until wilted.

17. Divide the sweet potatoes into the bowls.

18. Top with the turkey mixture, spinach and eggs.

19. Sprinkle the pistachios on top.

20. Serve with the hot sauce.

Nutritional Value:

- Calories 420
- Total Fat 19.7g
- Saturated Fat 3.9g
- Cholesterol 150mg
- Sodium 198mg

- Total Carbohydrate 42.6g
- Dietary Fiber 8.9g
- Total Sugars 7.1g
- Protein 22.5g
- Potassium 1770mg

Sweet Potato Hash

Preparation Time: 20 minutes

Cooking Time: 35 minutes

Servings: 2

Ingredients:

- 3 tablespoons olive oil
- 2 sweet potatoes, cubed
- ½ onion, diced
- 1 red bell pepper, diced
- ½ teaspoon garlic powder
- 1 teaspoon chili powder
- Salt and pepper to taste
- 2 fried eggs
- Cilantro
- Salsa

Method:

1. Preheat your oven to 400 degrees F.
2. Cover your baking pan with foil.
3. In a bowl, toss the sweet potato cubes, onion and red bell pepper in olive oil and spices. Coat evenly.
4. Spread the vegetables on the baking pan.
5. Bake for 35 minutes.
6. Top the hash with the fried egg and cilantro.
7. Serve with the salsa.

Nutritional Value:

- Calories 242
- Total Fat 14.1g
- Saturated Fat 2.3g
- Cholesterol 88mg
- Total Carbohydrate 25.1g
- Dietary Fiber 4g
- Total Sugars 2.6g
- Protein 4.7g
- Potassium 705mg

Potato & Broccoli Breakfast Bowl

Preparation Time: 45 minutes

Cooking Time: 25 minutes

Servings: 2-4

Ingredients:

- 4 tablespoons olive oil, divided
- 3 cloves garlic, minced
- 1 green bell pepper, diced
- 1 potato, cubed
- Salt and pepper to taste
- 1 cup broccoli florets
- 1 cup onion, sliced
- 2 cups baby spinach
- 1 avocado, sliced in half
- Sesame seeds
- 2 eggs, poached
- ½ cup crispy chickpeas

Method:

1. Pour 1 tablespoon olive oil in a skillet over medium low heat.
2. Add the garlic and bell pepper.
3. Cook for 1 minute.
4. Add the potato cubes.
5. Season with the salt and pepper.
6. Cook until brown and a little soft.
7. Set aside.
8. Pour 1 tablespoon olive oil into the same pan.
9. Add the broccoli.
10. Cook for 2 to 3 minutes.
11. Remove and transfer to a plate.
12. Add the remaining olive oil into the pan.
13. Add the onions and sauté for 5 minutes.
14. Lower the heat and cook for 30 more minutes, stirring occasionally.
15. Assemble the bowls by layering the spinach, potatoes, broccoli, and caramelized onions.
16. Put the avocado on one side and the poached eggs on the other.
17. Top with the crispy chickpeas and sesame seeds.

Nutritional Value:

- Calories 350
- Total Fat 18g
- Saturated Fat 2.9g
- Cholesterol 0mg
- Sodium 261mg

- Total Carbohydrate 41.2g
- Dietary Fiber 10.6g
- Total Sugars 4.3g
- Protein 9.6g
- Potassium 741mg

Oats & Banana

Preparation Time: 5 minutes

Cooking Time: 0 minute

Servings: 1

Ingredients:

- 1 ½ bananas
- 1 tablespoon almond butter
- 1 cup vanilla almond milk
- 2 tablespoons dark chocolate chips
- 1 tablespoon peanut butter
- ½ cup ice
- ½ cup rolled oats
- 3 tablespoons chia seeds
- 6 bananas round slices
- Slivered almonds

Method:

1. Put all the ingredients in a blender except the almonds and banana slices.
2. Pulse until creamy.
3. Pour the contents into a bowl.
4. Top with the banana slices and almonds.

Nutritional Value:

- Calories 213
- Total Fat 9.7g
- Saturated Fat 1.9g
- Cholesterol 0mg
- Sodium 78mg
- Total Carbohydrate 29.4g
- Dietary Fiber 4.9g
- Total Sugars 10.8g
- Protein 5.9g
- Potassium 399mg

Eggs & Quinoa

Preparation Time: 15 minutes
Cooking Time: 15 minutes
Servings: 2
Ingredients:

- 1 cup water
- ¼ cup quinoa
- 1 small avocado, sliced
- 2 eggs, poached
- ½ cup watercress leaves
- 1 bulb beetroot, sliced thinly
- 1 teaspoon apple cider vinegar
- 1 teaspoon lemon juice
- Salt and pepper to taste

Method:

1. Pour the water into a pan over medium heat.
2. Add the quinoa and let it absorb the water.
3. Cook for 15 minutes.
4. Place the quinoa in the bowl.
5. Add the avocado, egg, watercress and beetroot.
6. Mix the lemon juice, vinegar, salt and pepper.
7. Drizzle this mixture on top of the bowl before serving.

Nutritional Value:

- Calories 349
- Total Fat 25.3g
- Saturated Fat 5.7g
- Cholesterol 164mg
- Sodium 75mg
- Total Carbohydrate 22.8g
- Dietary Fiber 8.4g
- Total Sugars 0.9g
- Protein 10.7g
- Potassium 687mg

Sausage & Eggs

Preparation Time: 20 minutes
Cooking Time: 15 minutes
Servings: 2
Ingredients:

- 2 tablespoons ghee
- 1 cup cauliflower rice
- 2 cooked sausages, sliced
- 2 cups steamed greens
- 2 eggs, poached
- 1 cup avocado, cubed
- 1 cup cucumber, sliced
- Chopped onions
- Lemon wedges
- Fresh herbs

Method:

1. Place your skillet over medium heat.
2. Add the ghee.
3. Add the cauliflower rice and cook for 3 to 5 minutes.
4. Transfer the cauliflower rice to bowls.
5. Add the sausage to the same pan to reheat.
6. Place the sausage slices on top of the cauliflower rice.
7. Add the leafy greens, eggs, avocado cubes and cucumber.
8. Garnish with the chopped onion and lemon wedges.
9. Sprinkle fresh herbs on top before serving.

Nutritional Value:

- Calories 484
- Total Fat 40 g
- Saturated Fat 13 g
- Cholesterol 258 mg
- Sodium 233 mg
- Total Carbohydrates 13 g
- Fiber 8 g
- Total Sugars 2.5 g
- Protein 25 g
- Potassium 525 mg

Egg, Kale & Avocado Breakfast

Preparation Time: 10 minutes

Cooking Time: 15 minutes

Servings: 1

Ingredients:

- 1 cup cooked brown rice
- 1 sunny side up egg
- 1 cup avocado, cubed
- ½ cup cucumber slices
- 1 cup kale, steamed
- Salt and pepper to taste

Method:

1. Fill the bowl with cooked brown rice.
2. Arrange the avocado cubes and cucumber slices on one side.
3. Place the kale on the other side.
4. Top it with the sunny side up egg.
5. Season with the salt and pepper.

Nutritional Value:

- Calories 563
- Total Fat 20.3g
- Saturated Fat 4.5g
- Cholesterol 110mg
- Sodium 73mg
- Total Carbohydrate 83.1g
- Dietary Fiber 8.8g
- Total Sugars 0.8g
- Protein 13.2g
- Potassium 812mg

Baked Oats with Seeds & Coconut Flakes

Preparation Time: 10 minutes

Cooking Time: 45 minutes

Servings: 6

Ingredients:

- 1 tablespoon of coconut oil
- 2 cups rolled oats
- 1 tablespoon sunflower seeds
- 1 tablespoon pumpkin seeds
- ½ tablespoon chia seeds
- 2 ripe bananas, mashed
- 1 cup coconut flakes
- 1 tablespoon walnuts, chopped
- ½ teaspoon cinnamon
- Salt to taste

Method:

1. Preheat your oven to 300 degrees F.
2. Combine all the ingredients in a large bowl.
3. Let sit for 5 minutes.
4. Transfer the mixture to a greased baking pan.
5. Press down to make it compact.
6. Bake in the oven for 45 minutes (open every 15 minutes to mix it up.)
7. Let cool.
8. Transfer to bowl and top with fruit slices of your choice.

Nutritional Value:

- Calories 236
- Total Fat 11g
- Saturated Fat 6.5g
- Sodium 33mg
- Total Carbohydrate 31.1g
- Dietary Fiber 6.1g
- Total Sugars 5.9g
- Protein 5.6g
- Potassium 319mg

Mexican Breakfast Bowl

Preparation Time: 15 minutes
Cooking Time: 20 minutes
Servings: 4
Ingredients:

- 2 cups sweet potatoes, diced
- 1 onion, diced
- 2 tablespoons olive oil
- Pinch chili powder
- Salt and pepper to taste
- 2 cups cooked ground turkey
- 1 ½ cups cooked black beans
- 4 eggs, poached
- Avocado slices
- Sour cream
- Cilantro
- Hot sauce

Method:

1. Toss the sweet potatoes and onion in the olive oil.
2. Season with the chili powder, salt and pepper.
3. Place on a baking pan.
4. Bake in the oven at 400 degrees F for 20 minutes.
5. Transfer the sweet potatoes into four bowls.
6. Top with the turkey, black beans and poached eggs.
7. Serve with avocado slices, sour cream, cilantro and hot sauce.

Nutritional Value:

- Calories 554
- Total Fat 17.2g
- Saturated Fat 3.4g
- Total Carbohydrate 69.3g
- Dietary Fiber 14.8g
- Total Sugars 3.4g
- Protein 34.3g
- Potassium 1907mg

Chapter 6: Chicken Bowls

Chicken Teriyaki

Preparation Time: 15 minutes

Cooking Time: 45 minutes

Servings: 4

Ingredients:

- 3 cups water
- 1 ½ cups brown rice
- Salt to taste
- 20 oz. frozen teriyaki chicken
- 1 cup cabbage, shredded
- 1 cup carrots, shredded
- 16 snow pea pods
- 2 green onions, sliced
- 2 radishes, chopped
- ¼ cup sprouts

Method:

1. In a pot over medium heat, add the water, rice and salt.
2. Bring to a boil and then reduce to simmer until rice is cooked.
3. In a pan over medium high heat, cook the chicken for 6 to 8 minutes.
4. Add the teriyaki sauce.
5. Add the rice to serving bowls.
6. Top with the teriyaki chicken and the rest of the ingredients.

Nutritional Value:

- Calories 372
- Total Fat 2.9g
- Saturated Fat 0.7g
- Cholesterol 0mg
- Sodium 261mg
- Total Carbohydrate 74g
- Dietary Fiber 6.1g
- Total Sugars 6.5g
- Protein 12.3g
- Potassium 448mg

Korean Chicken

Preparation Time: 30 minutes
Cooking Time: 50 minutes
Servings: 6
Ingredients:

- ¼ cup kimchi juice
- 7 ounces yogurt
- 2 chicken breasts, sliced into cubes
- ½ cup bread crumbs
- 2 cups lettuce, shredded
- ¼ cup carrots, shredded
- ¼ cup cucumber, sliced into thin strips
- ¼ cup radish, sliced thinly
- 3 tablespoons kimchi
- 2 tablespoons rice wine vinegar
- 1 teaspoon ginger paste
- 2 tablespoons sesame oil
- 1 tablespoon sugar
- 2 tablespoons soy sauce
- Pepper to taste
- Sesame seeds
- 1 green onion

Method:

1. Mix the kimchi juice and yogurt in a bowl.
2. Marinate the chicken in this mixture for 1 hour covered in the refrigerator.
3. Cover the chicken cubes in bread crumbs.
4. Place the chicken in a greased baking pan.
5. Bake in the oven at 375 degrees F until golden brown.
6. Place the lettuce leaves on the bottom of the bowl.
7. Top with the chicken, carrots, cucumber, radish and kimchi.
8. In another bowl, blend the vinegar, ginger paste, sesame oil, sugar, soy sauce and pepper.
9. Pour this mixture on top of the bowl.
10. Sprinkle sesame seeds and green onion before serving.

Nutritional Value:

- Calories 431
- Total Fat 18.2g
- Saturated Fat 4.2g
- Cholesterol 91mg
- Sodium 990mg
- Total Carbohydrate 26.6g

- Dietary Fiber 1.8g
- Total Sugars 11.2g
- Protein 35.5g
- Potassium 588mg

Chicken with Broccoli & Quinoa

Preparation Time: 30 minutes
Cooking Time: 55 minutes
Servings: 2
Ingredients:

- ¼ cup uncooked quinoa
- 1 cup sweet potatoes, cubed
- 1 tablespoon sesame oil
- 1 clove garlic, minced
- 1 tablespoon soy sauce
- ¼ pound chicken breast (skinless), diced
- 1 cup broccoli florets, steamed
- 1 cup green beans, steamed
- 1 cup avocado, cubed
- ½ teaspoon sesame seeds

Method:

1. Preheat your oven to 350 degrees F.
2. Cook the quinoa according to package directions.
3. Toss the sweet potato in a little sesame oil.
4. Place in a greased baking sheet.
5. Bake in the oven for 15 minutes.
6. In a shallow dish, combine the garlic and soy sauce.
7. Marinate the chicken in this mixture for 30 minutes.
8. In a pan over medium heat, pour in the remaining sesame oil.
9. Cook the chicken for 6 to 10 minutes.
10. Assemble the bowls by adding the quinoa first.
11. Then top with the sweet potatoes, chicken, broccoli, green beans and avocado.
12. Garnish with the sesame seeds.

Nutritional Value:

- Calories 484
- Total Fat 24.5g
- Saturated Fat 4.2g
- Cholesterol 36mg
- Sodium 511mg
- Total Carbohydrate 49.1g
- Dietary Fiber 12.7g
- Total Sugars 2.5g
- Protein 20.6g
- Potassium 1581mg

Thai Chicken

Preparation Time: 20 minutes

Cooking Time: 30 minutes

Servings: 4

Ingredients:

- 1 cup farro
- ¼ cup chicken stock
- 1 tablespoon lime juice
- 1 tablespoon brown sugar
- 1 ½ tablespoons ground chili paste
- 1 tablespoon fish sauce
- 1 tablespoon cornstarch
- 1-pound chicken breast, sliced into cubes
- 1 tablespoon olive oil
- 2 cloves garlic, minced
- 1 tablespoon ginger, grated
- 1 shallot, minced
- Salt and pepper to taste
- 2 cups kale, shredded
- 1 cup bean sprouts
- 1 ½ cups cabbage, shredded
- ½ cup fresh cilantro leaves
- ¼ cup roasted peanuts
- 2 carrots, grated

For spicy sauce:

- 3 tablespoons peanut butter
- 2 tablespoons lime juice
- 1 tablespoon soy sauce
- 2 teaspoons brown sugar
- 2 teaspoons ground chili paste

Method:

1. Cook the farro according to package instructions. Set aside.
2. In a bowl, mix the chicken stock, lime juice, brown sugar and ground chili paste. Set aside.
3. In another bowl, combine the fish sauce and cornstarch.
4. Toss the chicken in the fish sauce mixture.
5. Pour the olive oil in a pan over medium heat.
6. Cook the chicken until golden brown.
7. Add the garlic, ginger and shallot.
8. Cook for 3 minutes.
9. Stir in the chicken stock.

10. Season with the salt and pepper.
11. Simmer for 2 to 3 minutes.
12. Divide the farro into bowls.
13. Top with the chicken and the rest of the ingredients.
14. Mix the sauce ingredients together and dilute with a little water.
15. Drizzle the spicy sauce over the Buddha bowl before serving.

Nutritional Value:

- Calories 503
- Total Fat 18 g
- Saturated Fat 3 g
- Cholesterol 68 mg
- Sodium 1103 mg
- Total Carbohydrates 61 g
- Fiber 4 g
- Total Sugars 6 g
- Protein 28 g
- Potassium 425 mg

Lemon Garlic Chicken with Sweet Potato Fries

Preparation Time: 40 minutes

Cooking Time: 40 minutes

Serving: 1

Ingredients:

- 1 clove garlic, minced
- ½ teaspoon parsley
- 1 teaspoon lemon juice
- 100 grams chicken breast, sliced thinly
- ½ tablespoon coconut oil
- 1 cup sweet potato, sliced into thin fries
- Salt and pepper to taste
- ½ teaspoon garlic powder
- 1 teaspoon olive oil for cooking
- 1 tablespoon honey
- ½ teaspoon Dijon mustard
- 1 tablespoon balsamic vinegar
- 1 cup leafy greens
- ½ cucumber, chopped
- ½ avocado, sliced
- 2 hard-boiled eggs
- 5 tomatoes, sliced in half

Method:

1. Mix the garlic, parsley and lemon juice.
2. Soak the chicken in this mixture for 30 minutes.
3. Preheat your oven to 400 degrees F.
4. Lightly grease your baking sheet.
5. In a bowl, toss the sweet potato fries in coconut oil.
6. Season with the salt, pepper and garlic powder.
7. Bake the fries in the oven for 30 minutes, turning once halfway through.
8. Pour the olive oil in a pan over medium heat.
9. Cook the chicken until golden brown.
10. Transfer to a plate and set aside.
11. In a bowl, mix the honey, mustard and vinegar. Set aside.
12. Assemble the bowl by putting the leafy greens on the bottom layer.
13. Add the sweet potatoes, tomatoes, cucumber, avocado and eggs.
14. Top with the chicken.
15. Drizzle the dressing on top.

Nutritional Value:

- Calories 967
- Total Fat 44.2g
- Saturated Fat 13.7g
- Cholesterol 391mg
- Sodium 517mg

- Total Carbohydrate 103.9g
- Dietary Fiber 25.9g
- Total Sugars 52.7g
- Protein 49.3g
- Potassium 3668mg

Peanut Chicken

Preparation Time: 20 minutes
Cooking Time: 30 minutes
Servings: 8
Ingredients:

- Water
- 1 cup quinoa
- 3 cups kale
- 2 cups bean sprouts
- 1 cup carrot, shredded
- 1 cup cucumber, sliced
- 1 cup cabbage, sliced
- 1 cup red pepper, sliced
- 2 tablespoons cilantro, chopped
- 1 pound cooked chicken, sliced into cubes
- ¼ cup peanuts, roasted and chopped
- ¼ cup green onions, sliced
- 1 cup peanut dressing

Method:

1. Add the water and quinoa in a pot.
2. Bring to a boil and then simmer to reduce heat.
3. Cook for 20 minutes.
4. Remove from heat and let sit for 5 minutes while covered.
5. Put the quinoa in a bowl.
6. Arrange the rest of the ingredients on top, placing the chicken, peanuts and green onion at the top most layer.
7. Drizzle with the peanut sauce.

Nutritional Value:

- Calories 356
- Total Fat 212 g
- Saturated Fat 4 g
- Cholesterol 42 mg
- Sodium 65 mg
- Total Carbohydrates 23 g
- Fiber 5 g
- Total Sugars 4 g
- Protein 21 g
- Potassium 424 mg

Chicken Marinara

Preparation Time: 10 minutes
Cooking Time: 40 minutes
Servings: 4
Ingredients:

- 4 chicken breast fillets, sliced into strips
- Garlic salt to taste
- 1 egg
- 1 cup breadcrumbs
- 1 teaspoon basil
- 2 teaspoons olive oil, divided
- 1 onion, chopped
- 1 cup tomato sauce
- Salt and pepper to taste
- 4 cups cooked whole wheat pasta
- ½ cup mozzarella cheese, shredded
- ¼ cup Parmesan cheese
- 1 cup corn kernels
- 1 cup Romaine lettuce, shredded

Method:

1. Season the chicken with the garlic salt.
2. In one bowl, beat the egg.
3. In another bowl, mix the breadcrumbs and basil.
4. Dip the chicken strips first in the egg and then covered with the breadcrumbs with herbs.
5. Grease a baking sheet with 1 teaspoon oil.
6. Bake the chicken in the oven until golden brown.
7. In a saucepan, pour the remaining oil.
8. Add the onion and sauté for 1 minute.
9. Add the tomato sauce.
10. Season with the salt and pepper.
11. Set aside.
12. Arrange the bowls by putting the cooked pasta first.
13. Top with the chicken strips, putting them on one side.
14. Pour the tomato sauce over the chicken.
15. Add the cheeses on top of the sauce.
16. Place the lettuce and corn on one side of the bowl.

Nutritional Value:

- Calories 549
- Total Fat 17.7g
- Saturated Fat 4.7g
- Cholesterol 174mg
- Sodium 707mg

- Total Carbohydrate 43.8g
- Dietary Fiber 5.1g
- Total Sugars 7.4g
- Protein 53g
- Potassium 846mg

Honey Garlic Chicken

Preparation Time: 10 minutes

Cooking Time: 20 minutes

Servings: 4

Ingredients:

- 1 tablespoon soy sauce
- ¼ cup apple cider vinegar, divided
- ¼ cup honey, divided
- 1 tablespoon olive oil
- 1-pound chicken breast (boneless, skinless), sliced thinly
- 4 cloves garlic, minced
- 2 cups cooked quinoa
- 2 cups broccoli florets, steamed
- 1 ripe avocado, sliced
- 1 cup carrot, shredded
- 1 cup cabbage, shredded
- ¼ cup olive oil
- 1 teaspoon grainy mustard
- Salt to taste
- ¼ cup pumpkin seeds, toasted

Method:

1. Mix the soy sauce, 1 tablespoon vinegar and 2 tablespoons honey in a bowl. Set aside.
2. Pour 1 tablespoon olive oil in a pan over medium heat.
3. Sauté the garlic for 1 minute.
4. Add the chicken and cook until brown on both sides.
5. Pour in the honey mixture.
6. Reduce heat.
7. Simmer for 3 to 5 minutes.
8. Divide the quinoa among the bowls.
9. Top with the chicken, broccoli, avocado, carrot and cabbage.
10. In a bowl, mix the remaining vinegar, remaining honey, mustard, ¼ cup olive oil, mustard and salt.
11. Pour this sauce over the bowls.
12. Sprinkle with the pumpkin seeds on top.

Nutritional Value:

- Calories 712
- Total Fat 25.3g

- Saturated Fat 3.9g
- Cholesterol 73mg
- Sodium 361mg
- Total Carbohydrate 83.1g
- Dietary Fiber 10.9g
- Total Sugars 19.8g
- Protein 40.1g
- Potassium 1372mg

Roasted Chicken with Chili Mango Sauce

Preparation Time: 50 minutes

Cooking Time: 45 minutes

Servings: 2

Ingredients:

- 2 cups mango, cubed and divided
- 1 tablespoon apple cider vinegar
- 1 teaspoon honey
- 2 tablespoons coconut milk
- 1 teaspoon chili paste
- 1 cup sweet potato, cubed
- 1 ½ cup broccoli florets
- 3 tablespoons olive oil
- 1 cup cooked brown rice
- 1 ½ cups roasted chicken, shredded
- 1 cup baby spinach

Method:

1. Put 1 cup mango cubes, apple cider vinegar, honey, coconut milk and red pepper flakes in a food processor.
2. Blend until smooth. Set aside.
3. In a large bowl, toss the sweet potatoes and broccoli in olive oil.
4. Bake in the oven for 45 minutes.
5. Place the cooked rice in the bowls.
6. Top with the roasted broccoli and sweet potato and roasted chicken.
7. Add the baby spinach and remaining mango cubes.
8. Drizzle the chili mango sauce on top.

Nutritional Value:

- Calories 497
- Total Fat 18.2g
- Saturated Fat 4.5g
- Cholesterol 47mg
- Sodium 99mg
- Total Carbohydrate 63.8g
- Dietary Fiber 5.8g
- Total Sugars 17.2g
- Protein 21.9g
- Potassium 804mg

Chapter 7: Beef and Lamb Bowls

Lamb with Miso Ginger Sauce

Preparation Time: 15 minutes

Cooking Time: 25 minutes

Servings: 4

Ingredients:

- 1 clove garlic, chopped
- 1 tablespoon ginger, minced
- ¼ cup cashews, soaked overnight and drained
- 2 tablespoons miso paste
- ¼ cup rice vinegar
- 1 ½ teaspoons sesame oil
- 2 tablespoons water
- 1 teaspoon honey
- 2 tablespoons avocado oil
- 1-pound ground lamb
- Salt and pepper to taste
- 1 tablespoon coconut amino
- ¼ cup basil leaves, chopped
- 16 ounces broccoli rice
- 1 cup bok choy, sliced thinly, cooked
- 4 scallions, sliced thinly
- Bean sprouts

Method:

1. Place the garlic, ginger, cashews, miso paste, rice vinegar, sesame oil, water and honey in the food processor.
2. Pulse until smooth.
3. Pour the avocado oil in a pan over medium heat.
4. Cook the ground lamb until brown.
5. Season with the salt and pepper.
6. Stir in the coconut amino and basil.
7. Cook for 1 more minute.
8. Remove and set aside.
9. Heat the rice broccoli on the same pan.
10. Season with the salt and pepper.
11. Divide the rice among the 4 bowls.
12. Top with the ground lamb mixture, bok choy, scallions and bean sprouts.

13. Drizzle the ginger miso sauce on top before serving.

Nutritional Value:

- Calories 347
- Total Fat 15.8g
- Saturated Fat 4.3g
- Cholesterol 102mg
- Sodium 430mg

- Total Carbohydrate 12.3g
- Dietary Fiber 1.8g
- Total Sugars 3g
- Protein 36.9g
- Potassium 667mg

Beef Bruschetta

Preparation Time: 20 minutes

Cooking Time: 8 hours

Servings: 4

Ingredients:

- 2 onions, chopped
- 5 cloves garlic, peeled
- 4 beef chops
- 1 cup beef broth
- ¼ cup hoisin sauce
- 4 cups fresh spinach
- 1 cup tomatoes, chopped
- 1 teaspoon balsamic vinegar reduction
- 1 teaspoon olive oil
- 1 tablespoon fresh basil leaves, chopped
- ½ cup cooked farro
- 1 cup feta cheese, crumbled
- Salt and pepper to taste

Method:

1. Arrange the chopped onions on the bottom of a slow cooker.
2. Add the garlic cloves.
3. Place the beef chops on top.
4. Pour the broth and hoisin sauce on top.
5. Seal the pot.
6. Cook on low for 8 hours.
7. Let sit for 30 minutes before taking out of the pot.
8. Shred the beef using 2 forks.
9. Place the spinach on the bottom of the bowls.
10. Add the shredded beef on top.
11. In another bowl, coat the tomatoes with a mixture of the vinegar, olive oil and basil.
12. Add the tomatoes beside the shredded beef.
13. Add the farro and feta cheese.
14. Season with the salt and pepper before serving.

Nutritional Value:

- Calories 468
- Total Fat 23.1g

- Saturated Fat 13g
- Cholesterol 93mg
- Sodium 897mg
- Total Carbohydrate 37.2g

- Dietary Fiber 5.9g
- Total Sugars 19.5g
- Protein 29.7g
- Potassium 1142mg

Lamb with Salsa Verde

Preparation Time: 30 minutes

Cooking Time: 40 minutes

Servings: 4

Ingredients:

- 2 sweet potatoes, sliced into wedges
- 2 tablespoons olive oil, divided
- Pepper to taste
- 4 lamb leg steaks
- 2 tablespoons balsamic vinegar
- 1 tablespoon Dijon mustard
- 4 tablespoons olive oil
- ½ onion, chopped
- 1 clove garlic, crushed
- 1 teaspoon fresh coriander, chopped
- 1 tablespoon fresh mint, chopped
- 4 cups baby spinach leaves
- 1 cup cherry tomatoes
- 1 cup chickpeas, rinsed and drained
- 1 cup baby beetroot, sliced and cooked
- 1 cup broccoli florets, blanched
- 1 cup feta cheese

Method:

1. Preheat your oven to 375 degrees F.
2. Toss the sweet potatoes in half of the olive oil.
3. Season with the pepper.
4. Place the sweet potatoes on a baking sheet.
5. Bake in the oven for 20 minutes or until tender and crisp.
6. Brush the lamb legs with the remaining oil.
7. Sprinkle the pepper on each side.
8. Grill the lamb steaks for 7 minutes per side.
9. Let sit for 10 minutes before slicing into strips.
10. In a bowl, mix the vinegar, mustard, olive oil, onion, garlic, coriander and mint. Set aside.
11. Arrange the bowls by placing the sweet potato wedges on the bottom.
12. Add the spinach leaves and the rest of the ingredients.

13. Top with the lamb strips and drizzle with the salsa before serving.

Nutritional Value:

- Calories 536
- Total Fat 21.3g
- Saturated Fat 7.8g
- Cholesterol 164mg
- Sodium 382mg

- Total Carbohydrate 29.5g
- Dietary Fiber 7.1g
- Total Sugars 4.8g
- Protein 55.1g
- Potassium 1278mg

Steak & Quinoa

Preparation Time: 15 minutes
Cooking Time: 15 minutes
Servings: 2
Ingredients:

- ¼ cup quinoa (uncooked)
- ½ tablespoon olive oil
- 2 scallions, chopped
- 4 ounces Swiss chard, sliced
- 2 ounces cooked steak
- 1 ounce roasted sweet potatoes
- 1 tablespoon raisins
- 1 tablespoon olive oil
- 2 teaspoons lemon juice
- 2 teaspoons tahini
- 1 teaspoon honey

Method:

1. Cook the quinoa according to package directions.
2. Remove from heat and set aside.
3. In a pan over medium heat, pour in the olive oil.
4. Heat the Swiss chard and scallions.
5. Cook until soft.
6. Put the quinoa in the bowl with the chard.
7. Add the steak, roasted sweet potatoes and raisins.
8. In another bowl, mix the olive oil, lemon juice, tahini and honey.
9. Drizzle this mixture over the steak and vegetables.

Nutritional Value:

- Calories 320
- Total Fat 18 g
- Saturated Fat 3 g
- Cholesterol 17 mg
- Sodium 150 mg
- Total Carbohydrates 29 g
- Dietary Fiber 3 g
- Total Sugars 4 g
- Protein 11 g
- Potassium 576 mg

Salisbury Steak

Preparation Time: 10 minutes
Cooking Time: 20 minutes
Servings: 4
Ingredients:

- 4 cups ground beef
- 1 onion, chopped
- 1 bell pepper, chopped
- 3 tablespoons parsley, chopped
- 1 egg, beaten
- ¼ cup breadcrumbs
- 1 tablespoon almond milk
- Salt and pepper to taste
- 3 tablespoons olive oil
- 1 ½ cups low sodium gravy
- ¼ cup mushrooms, sliced
- 4 cups brown rice
- 4 cups lettuce
- 1 cup cucumber, sliced into rounds
- 1 cup tomatoes, sliced into rounds

Method:

1. Make the Salisbury steak by mixing the ground beef, onion, bell pepper, parsley, egg, breadcrumbs and almond milk.
2. Season with the salt and pepper.
3. In a skillet over medium heat, pour in the olive oil and cook the patties until brown on both sides.
4. Remove the patties and set aside.
5. Put the mushrooms on the same pan.
6. Heat through for 1 minute.
7. Add the mushrooms to the gravy.
8. Place the brown rice in the bowl.
9. Add the Salisbury steak on top.
10. Pour the gravy on top of the steak.
11. On the side, arrange the lettuce, cucumber and tomatoes.

Nutritional Value:

- Calories 910
- Total Fat 19.6g
- Saturated Fat 4.3g
- Cholesterol 60mg

- Sodium 96mg
- Total Carbohydrate 159.4g
- Dietary Fiber 9g

- Total Sugars 5.6g
- Protein 24.7g
- Potassium 981mg

Grilled Beef with Asparagus & Avocado

Preparation Time: 20 minutes
Cooking Time: 15 minutes
Servings: 4
Ingredients:

- 1-pound beef rump steak
- 2 teaspoons sesame oil
- 1 cup asparagus, trimmed
- 1 teaspoon olive oil
- 2 tablespoons lime juice
- 2 tablespoons soy sauce
- 1 tablespoon brown sugar
- 4 cups cooked brown rice
- 1 avocado, sliced thinly
- 1 cucumber, sliced into thin sticks
- 4 cups baby rocket leaves
- 1 cup cherry tomatoes, sliced in half
- 2 teaspoons sesame seeds, toasted

Method:

1. Preheat your barbecue grill.
2. Coat the beef in sesame oil.
3. Grill for 3 minutes per side.
4. Let sit for 5 minutes before slicing. Set aside.
5. Grill the asparagus for 2 minutes, turning once.
6. In a bowl, mix the olive oil, lime juice, soy sauce and brown sugar. Set aside.
7. Place the brown rice in the bowls.
8. Top with the grilled beef and asparagus.
9. Arrange the avocado, cucumber, rocket leaves and cherry tomatoes on the same layer.
10. Sprinkle the sesame seeds on top.

Nutritional Value:

- Calories 636
- Total Fat 16.1g
- Saturated Fat 2.5g
- Cholesterol 0mg
- Sodium 311mg
- Total Carbohydrate 105.3g
- Dietary Fiber 7.8g
- Total Sugars 3.8g
- Protein 18.5g
- Potassium 710mg

Flank Stew with Cashew Sauce

Preparation Time: 30 minutes
Cooking Time: 35 minutes
Servings: 4
Ingredients:

- 4 broccolini stalks
- 1 cup sweet potatoes, chopped
- 3 tablespoons avocado oil
- 1 tablespoon sesame oil
- 1 teaspoon garlic, minced
- ½ pound flank steak, sliced thinly
- 1 teaspoon sesame seeds
- ¼ cup cashew butter
- 4 tablespoons coconut amino
- ¼ cup coconut milk
- 1 tablespoon curry paste
- 1 cup barley, cooked
- ½ cup lentils, cooked
- 1 cup carrot, shredded
- 1 cup spinach, steamed
- 2 tablespoons sprouts
- ¼ cup red cabbage
- 2 eggs, poached
- Salt and pepper to taste

Method:

1. Preheat your oven to 400 degrees F.
2. Arrange the broccolini and sweet potatoes on a baking pan.
3. Coat evenly with the avocado oil.
4. Season with the salt and pepper.
5. Bake in the oven for 20 minutes.
6. In a skillet over medium high heat, pour in the sesame oil.
7. Cook the garlic for 1 minute.
8. Add the beef and sesame seeds and cook for 10 minutes, stirring occasionally.
9. In a bowl, mix the cashew butter, coconut amino, coconut milk and curry paste.
10. Divide the barley among 4 bowls.
11. Add the beef and the rest of the ingredients on top.
12. Season with the salt and pepper.

Nutritional Value:

11. Calories 556
- Total Fat 19.2g
- Saturated Fat 6.9g
- Cholesterol 113mg

- Sodium 101mg
- Total Carbohydrate 65g
- Dietary Fiber 18.7g
- Total Sugars 3.3g
- Protein 32.4g
- Potassium 1181mg

Beef Shawarma

Preparation Time: 15 minutes
Cooking Time: 20 minutes
Servings: 4
Ingredients:

- 1 tablespoon olive oil
- 8 cups steak, thinly sliced
- Salt and pepper to taste
- 1 teaspoon dried basil
- ½ cup mayonnaise
- ¼ cup water
- 1 tablespoon garlic, minced
- Garlic salt to taste
- 4 cups cooked brown rice
- 2 cups cucumber, sliced into strips
- 2 cups tomatoes, chopped
- 2 cups cabbage, shredded
- 1 cup white onion, chopped

Method:

1. In a skillet over medium heat, pour in the olive oil.
2. Season the beef with the salt and pepper.
3. Add the beef and cook until brown on both sides.
4. Sprinkle the dried basil on the beef.
5. Remove from heat and set aside.
6. In a bowl, mix the mayonnaise, water, garlic and garlic salt. Set aside.
7. Assemble the bowls by putting the brown rice on the bottom.
8. Arrange the beef on one side and the cucumbers, tomatoes, cabbage and white onion on the other.
9. Drizzle with the mayo mixture before serving.

Nutritional Value:

- Calories 635
- Total Fat 14.3g
- Saturated Fat 3.2g
- Cholesterol 92mg
- Sodium 159mg
- Total Carbohydrate 81.3g
- Dietary Fiber 4.7g
- Total Sugars 3.7g
- Protein 43.6g
- Potassium 784mg

Asian Beef Bowl

Preparation Time: 20 minutes
Cooking Time: 20 minutes
Servings: 4
Ingredients:

- 1 teaspoon sesame oil
- ¼ cup soy sauce
- 2 teaspoons brown sugar
- 2 tablespoons water
- ½ teaspoon red pepper flakes, crushed
- Cooking spray
- 1-pound lean ground beef
- 2 cloves garlic, crushed
- ¼ cup onion, chopped
- 1 teaspoon ginger, grated
- 3 cups cooked brown rice
- ½ cucumber, sliced
- 2 scallions, sliced
- ½ tablespoon sesame seeds

Method:

1. In a small bowl, mix the sesame oil, soy sauce, brown sugar, water and red pepper flakes. Set aside.
2. Spray a pan with oil and put on a stove.
3. Add the ground beef and cook for 5 minutes.
4. Add the garlic, onion and ginger.
5. Cook for 1 more minute, stirring frequently.
6. Pour the sesame oil mixture over the beef.
7. Reduce the heat and simmer for 10 minutes.
8. Assemble the bowls by dividing the rice among 4 bowls.
9. Top each with beef, cucumber, scallions and sesame seeds.

Nutritional Value:

- Calories 394
- Total Fat 9 g
- Saturated Fat 3 g
- Cholesterol 70 mg
- Sodium 807 mg
- Total Carbohydrates 47 g

- Dietary Fiber 4 g
- Total Sugars 7 g
- Protein 30 g
- Potassium 457 mg

Lamb Biryani with Tomato Salad

Preparation Time: 30 minutes
Cooking Time: 25 minutes
Servings: 2
Ingredients:

- 1 tablespoon coconut oil
- 1 cup white onion, sliced
- 1 Thai chili, minced
- ½ pound ground lamb
- 1 teaspoon garlic, grated
- 1 teaspoon ginger, grated
- ½ cup carrots, grated
- 15 ounces garbanzo beans
- Salt to taste
- ½ teaspoon cayenne
- 1 teaspoon cumin
- ½ teaspoon coriander
- ¼ teaspoon Garam Masala
- 1/8 teaspoon turmeric
- ½ teaspoon fresh cilantro, chopped
- 3 tablespoons and 1 teaspoon lime juice, divided
- 1 cup tomato, chopped
- ¼ cup red onion, diced
- 2 teaspoons mint, chopped
- 4 cups cauliflower rice

Method:

1. In a skillet over medium heat, pour in the oil.
2. Add the white onion and chili.
3. Cook for 8 minutes.
4. Add the ground lamb and cook until brown.
5. Add the garlic, ginger, carrots, garbanzo beans
6. Add the salt, cayenne, cumin, coriander, Garam masala, turmeric and cilantro
7. Stir in the 1 teaspoon lime juice.
8. Simmer for 3 minutes.
9. In a bowl, mix the tomato, red onion, mint and remaining lime juice.
10. Arrange the bowl by putting the cauliflower rice on the bottom.

11. Top with the cooked lamb with vegetables.
12. Place the salad on the side.

Nutritional Value:

- Calories 553
- Total Fat 14.3g
- Saturated Fat 5.1g
- Cholesterol 51mg
- Sodium 122mg

- Total Carbohydrate 71.3g
- Dietary Fiber 20.3g
- Total Sugars 14.5g
- Protein 37.5g
- Potassium 1342mg

Chapter 8: Vegetable Bowls

Spring Broccoli

Preparation Time: 30 minutes
Cooking Time: 40 minutes
Servings: 4
Ingredients:

- 2 cups broccoli florets
- 2 sweet potatoes, sliced into wedges
- 2 tablespoons olive oil
- Salt and pepper to taste
- 2 cups purple cabbage, shredded
- 1 tablespoon lemon juice
- 4 cups cooked brown rice
- 1 cup cooked green lentils
- 2 carrots, shredded
- 1 avocado, sliced
- 1 orange, sliced
- Sprouts
- 2 tablespoons sesame seeds

For the sauce:

- 1 clove garlic, smashed
- 1 ginger, peeled
- ½ cup roasted cashews
- 1 tablespoon maple syrup
- 1 tablespoon apple cider vinegar
- ½ teaspoon ground turmeric
- 1 tablespoon lemon juice
- Pinch cayenne pepper
- Salt and pepper to taste

Method:

1. Preheat your oven to 425 degrees F.
2. Prepare two baking sheets.
3. On the first one, place the sweet potatoes.
4. On the other one, arrange the broccoli florets.
5. Coat both vegetables with the olive oil and season with the salt and pepper.
6. Bake each in the oven for 20 minutes.
7. Make the sauce by placing all the sauce ingredients in a food processor.
8. Assemble the bowls by dividing the rice and lentils and placing them on the bottom part.
9. Top with the roasted vegetables and the rest of the ingredients.

10. Sprinkle sesame seeds and pour the dressing on top.

Nutritional Value:

- Calories 654
- Total Fat 16.6g
- Saturated Fat 3.1g
- Cholesterol 0mg
- Sodium 34mg

- Total Carbohydrate 111.5g
- Dietary Fiber 16.3g
- Total Sugars 6.7g
- Protein 17.4g
- Potassium 1180mg

Avocado, Arugula & Quinoa

Preparation Time: 30 minutes

Cooking Time: 15 minutes

Servings: 1

Ingredients:

- ½ cup cooked quinoa
- 1 cup arugula
- 1 cup Brussels sprouts, sautéed
- 1 tablespoon pepitas
- ½ cup avocado, sliced
- 1 teaspoon olive oil
- 1 tablespoon tahini
- Salt and pepper to taste

Method:

1. Assemble the bowl by placing the quinoa on the bottom.
2. Top with the arugula, Brussels sprouts, pepitas and avocado.
3. In another bowl, mix the olive oil, tahini, salt and pepper.
4. Drizzle this mixture over the bowl and serve.

Nutritional Value:

- Calories 634
- Total Fat 32.6g
- Saturated Fat 5.5g
- Cholesterol 0mg
- Sodium 54mg
- Total Carbohydrate 72.8g
- Dietary Fiber 15.9g
- Total Sugars 2.8g
- Protein 19.5g
- Potassium 1312mg

Rainbow Bowl

Preparation Time: 20 minutes
Cooking Time: 40 minutes
Servings: 4
Ingredients:

- 1 cup delicata squash, sliced thinly
- 1 cup butternut squash, cubed
- 1 cup button mushrooms
- Cooking spray
- 2 tablespoons liquid amino, divided
- Salt and pepper to taste
- 1 teaspoon dried rosemary
- 1 teaspoon dried thyme
- 2 cups great northern white beans
- ½ cup tahini
- 2 tablespoons maple syrup
- 3 tablespoons lemon juice
- ¼ cup almond milk
- ½ teaspoon ground ginger
- ¼ teaspoon garlic powder
- 4 cup cooked wild rice
- 4 cups leafy greens
- 1 cup avocado, diced
- 1 cup pickled cabbage

Method:

1. Preheat the oven to 425 degrees F.
2. Prepare two baking pans.
3. Place the delicata squash and butternut squash on 1 pan.
4. Place the mushrooms on the other pan.
5. Spray oil on both sets of veggies.
6. Toss the mushrooms in half of the liquid amino.
7. Season both vegetables with salt, pepper, rosemary and thyme.
8. Bake the squash in the oven for 25 minutes.
9. Bake the mushrooms for 15 minutes.
10. Meanwhile, heat the beans in a skillet over medium heat.
11. Add the remaining liquid amino.
12. Season with the pepper.

13. In a small bowl, mix the tahini, maple syrup, lemon juice, milk, ginger and garlic powder.
14. Fill the bowls with the rice, roasted vegetables, beans, greens, avocado and pickled cabbage.
15. Pour the tahini sauce on top.

Nutritional Value:

- Calories 456
- Total Fat 14.5g
- Saturated Fat 3.7g
- Cholesterol 0mg
- Sodium 28mg
- Total Carbohydrate 71.2g
- Dietary Fiber 8.3g
- Total Sugars 6.1g
- Protein 15.4g
- Potassium 624mg

Curried Chickpeas

Preparation Time: 10 minutes
Cooking Time: 25 minutes
Servings: 2
Ingredients:

- 2 cups chickpeas, rinsed and drained
- 2 tablespoons olive oil
- Salt to taste
- 1 teaspoon curry powder
- 2 cups cooked quinoa
- 1 cup roasted sweet potatoes
- 1 cup roasted broccoli florets
- 1 cup grilled asparagus
- ¼ cup hummus

Method:

1. Preheat your oven to 400 degrees F.
2. Dry the chickpeas with paper towel.
3. Place the chickpeas on a baking sheet.
4. Toss them in olive oil and salt.
5. Bake in the oven for 25 minutes.
6. Season with the curry powder.
7. Divide the quinoa among 2 bowls.
8. Top with the sweet potatoes, broccoli, asparagus and chickpeas.
9. Serve with the hummus.

Nutritional Value:

- Calories 612
- Total Fat 15.8g
- Saturated Fat 2g
- Sodium 101mg
- Potassium 1118mg
- Total Carbohydrate 94.2g
- Dietary Fiber 19.6g
- Total Sugars 8.6g
- Protein 26.1g

Roasted Veggies & Cauliflower Rice

Preparation Time: 15 minutes

Cooking Time: 25 minutes

Servings: 6

Ingredients:

- 6 cups cauliflower rice
- 2 tablespoons avocado oil
- 8 ounces Brussels sprouts, sliced in half
- 1 red bell pepper, sliced into strips
- 1 sweet potato, diced
- ¼ cup pecans, chopped
- Salt and pepper to taste

For the dressing:

- 1 avocado
- 2 cloves garlic
- 2 tablespoons apple cider vinegar
- 1 teaspoon cumin
- ¼ cup lime juice
- ½ cup water
- ¼ cup fresh cilantro, chopped
- ¼ cup pumpkin seeds
- 1 teaspoon salt
- ½ cup olive oil

Method:

1. Preheat your oven to 425 degrees F.
2. Grease a baking pan.
3. Coat the Brussels sprouts, red bell pepper and sweet potato in avocado oil.
4. Bake in the oven for 25 minutes.
5. While waiting, blend the sauce ingredients in a food processor.
6. Arrange the bowls by placing the cauliflower rice on the bottom.
7. Top with the roasted vegetables.
8. Season with the salt and pepper.
9. Pour the dressing and sprinkle pecans on top before serving.

Nutritional Value:

- Calories 376
- Total Fat 34 g
- Saturated Fat 4 g
- Cholesterol 0 mg
- Sodium 444 mg
- Total Carbohydrates 16 g
- Fiber 7 g
- Total Sugars 5 g

- Protein 6 g
- Potassium 834 mg

Red Cabbage in Garlic Sauce

Preparation Time: 15 minutes
Cooking Time: 0 minute
Servings: 2
Ingredients:

- 3 cups brown rice, cooked
- 1 cup red cabbage, shredded
- 1 avocado, sliced thinly
- 1 cup carrot, shredded
- 1 cup cherry tomatoes, sliced in half
- ¼ cup green onion, sliced thinly

For the dressing:

- 4 cloves garlic, peeled
- ½ cup olive oil
- Salt and pepper to taste
- 1 tablespoon Dijon mustard
- 2 tablespoons lemon juice
- ½ teaspoon onion powder
- 2 tablespoons water

Method:

1. Prepare the sauce by blending the dressing ingredients in a food processor. Set aside.
2. Arrange the bowls by dividing the cooked rice and topping with the rest of the ingredients.
3. Pour the sauce over the vegetables before serving.

Nutritional Value:

- Calories 455
- Total Fat 12 g
- Saturated Fat 3 g
- Sodium 226 mg
- Total Carbohydrates 14 g
- Total Sugars 12 g
- Protein 2 g
- Potassium 566 mg

Cauliflower & Spinach with Falafel

Preparation Time: 20 minutes

Cooking Time: 40 minutes

Servings: 4

Ingredients:

- 4 carrots, sliced into strips
- 1 head cauliflower, chopped into florets
- 2 tablespoons olive oil
- Salt and pepper to taste
- 4 teaspoons cumin
- 8 pieces baked falafel
- 2 cups spinach, chopped
- 1 cup red cabbage, chopped
- 1 jalapeño pepper, sliced
- 1 tablespoon honey
- ¼ cup pistachios, crushed

Method:

1. Preheat your oven to 400 degrees F.
2. Put the carrots and cauliflower florets on two different baking pans.
3. Drizzle each with oil and season with the salt, pepper and cumin.
4. Bake in the oven for 20 minutes.
5. Arrange the falafel, roasted carrots and cauliflower, spinach, cabbage and jalapeño pepper in the bowls.
6. Drizzle with the honey and top with the pistachios.

Nutritional Value:

- Calories 282
- Total Fat 17.5 g
- Saturated Fat 5 g
- Cholesterol 0 mg
- Sodium 192.7 mg
- Total Carbohydrates 26.5 g
- Dietary Fiber 5 g
- Total Sugars 6.4 g
- Protein 9.1 g

Roasted Veggies with Lemon Herb Cream Sauce

Preparation Time: 10 minutes
Cooking Time: 30 minutes
Serving: 1
Ingredients:

- ½ cup cooked chickpeas
- 1 cup carrots, sliced into strips
- 1 cup sweet potatoes, sliced into cubes

- 1 cup zucchini, sliced into rounds
- 2 tablespoons vegetable broth
- Salt and pepper to taste
- 1 cup cooked wild rice

For the dressing:

- 1 ½ cup cashew milk
- ¾ cup raw almonds
- 1 clove garlic
- 6 tablespoons lemon juice
- 1 teaspoon hot sauce

- 2 teaspoons apple cider vinegar
- ¼ cup cilantro, chopped
- ¼ cup chives, chopped
- ¼ cup parsley, chopped

Method:

1. Preheat your oven to 400 degrees F.
2. Cook the chickpeas according to directions.
3. Coat the vegetables with the broth, salt and pepper.
4. Bake in the oven for 15 minutes, shaking to cook evenly.
5. Make the dressing by blending the ingredients in a food processor.
6. Fill the bowl with the wild rice.
7. Top with the roasted vegetables and drizzle with the cream sauce before serving.

Nutritional Value:

- Calories 643
- Total Fat 11 g
- Saturated Fat 0 g
- Cholesterol 0 mg
- Sodium 428 mg

- Total Carbohydrates 119 g
- Dietary Fiber 13 g
- Total Sugars 3 g
- Protein 29 g
- Potassium 10 mg

Spring Veggies

Preparation Time: 20 minutes

Cooking Time: 15 minutes

Servings: 4

Ingredients:

- 3 tablespoons lemon juice
- 2 tablespoons tahini
- 2 tablespoons water
- ½ teaspoon ground turmeric
- ¼ teaspoon hot pepper sauce
- ½ teaspoon maple syrup
- Salt and pepper to taste
- 2 tablespoons olive oil
- 2 cups zucchini, sliced
- 2 cups asparagus, sliced
- 2 cups cooked quinoa
- 2 cups chickpeas, rinsed and drained
- 2 cups baby spinach
- 2 cups cherry tomatoes
- 2 tablespoons sesame seeds
- 1 cup fresh sprouts

Method:

1. Preheat your oven to 425 degrees F.
2. Grease a baking sheet.
3. Place the lemon juice, tahini, water, turmeric, hot sauce, maple syrup, salt and pepper in a food processor.
4. Pulse until creamy, slowly adding in a little olive oil.
5. Set aside.
6. Coat the zucchini and asparagus with the remaining olive oil.
7. Place on the baking sheet and bake for 15 minutes, turning once.
8. Arrange the bowls by placing the quinoa on the bottom.
9. Top with the roasted vegetables and the rest of the ingredients.
10. Pour the sauce over the veggies and serve.

Nutritional Value:

- Calories 440
- Total Fat 21 g
- Saturated Fat 3 g
- Cholesterol 0 mg
- Sodium 347 mg
- Total Carbohydrates 49 g
- Dietary Fiber 12 g
- Total Sugars 9 g

- Protein 17 g

- Potassium 878 mg

Chapter 9: Fruit Bowls

Fruit & Yogurt

Preparation Time: 10 minutes

Cooking Time: 0 minute

Serving: 1

Ingredients:

- 1 cup yogurt
- 2 tablespoons chia seeds
- 1 cup strawberries, sliced in half
- 1 cup apple, cubed
- 1 cup blueberries, sliced in half
- 1 tablespoons hemp seeds

Method:

1. Mix the yogurt and hemp seeds.
2. Let sit for 10 minutes.
3. Place the yogurt mixture in a serving bowl.
4. Arrange fruits on top and sprinkle with the hemp seeds.

Nutritional Value:

- Calories 538
- Total Fat 13.4g
- Saturated Fat 3.1g
- Cholesterol 15mg
- Sodium 177mg
- Total Carbohydrate 84.1g
- Dietary Fiber 14.7g
- Total Sugars 61.9g
- Protein 22.8g
- Potassium 1313mg

Mango & Avocado with Wasabi Dressing

Preparation Time: 15 minutes
Cooking Time: 20 minutes
Servings: 2
Ingredients:

- 1 cup dried roasted buckwheat groats
- 2 cups vegetable stock
- 2 cups cooked chickpeas
- 2 tablespoons soy sauce
- 1 teaspoon wasabi paste
- 1 teaspoon lime juice
- 1 tablespoon mirin
- 1 avocado, sliced
- 1 mango, sliced
- 3 spring onions, chopped
- 2 red peppers, diced

Method:

1. Put the groats in a pan over medium heat.
2. Add the vegetable stock.
3. Simmer for 15 minutes or until stock is absorbed.
4. While waiting, sauté the chickpeas in a skillet.
5. Make the dressing by combining the soy sauce, wasabi, lime juice and mirin.
6. Assemble the bowls putting the groats as the first layer.
7. Add the chickpeas on top.
8. Top with the avocado, mango and red peppers.
9. Pour the wasabi dressing on top.
10. Sprinkle with the spring onions.

Nutritional Value:

- Calories 584
- Total Fat 16.9g
- Saturated Fat 2.8g
- Cholesterol 0mg
- Sodium 529mg
- Total Carbohydrate 91.5g
- Dietary Fiber 24.1g
- Total Sugars 25.6g
- Protein 23.6g
- Potassium 1418mg

Mango & Avocado with Quinoa

Preparation Time: 15 minutes
Cooking Time: 20 minutes
Servings: 2
Ingredients:

- 2/3 cup dry quinoa
- 1 teaspoon chipotle powder
- 2 teaspoons onion powder
- 1 teaspoon garlic powder
- 1 1/3 cup water
- Salt to taste
- 1 avocado, cubed
- 1 mango, cubed
- 2 cups cooked black beans
- ½ cup kale, chopped and steamed
- 2/3 cup cilantro, chopped
- 1 teaspoon lime juice

Method:

1. In a pot, put the dry quinoa, chipotle powder, onion powder, garlic powder, water and salt.
2. Bring to a boil.
3. Cover, reduce heat and simmer for 15 minutes.
4. Place the quinoa in serving bowls.
5. Arrange the rest of the ingredients except the lime juice on top of the quinoa.
6. Drizzle the lime juice on top of the fruits.

Nutritional Value:

- Calories 599
- Total Fat 13.3g
- Saturated Fat 2.7g
- Cholesterol 0mg
- Sodium 57mg
- Total Carbohydrate 98g
- Dietary Fiber 21.8g
- Total Sugars 14.4g
- Protein 27.1g
- Potassium 2058mg

Watermelon, Berries & Yogurt

Preparation Time: 20 minutes

Cooking Time: 0 minute

Servings: 4

Ingredients:

- 4 cups yogurt
- 1 cup watermelon, cubed
- 1 cup pineapple chunks
- 4 cups grapes, sliced in half
- 4 cups strawberries, sliced in half
- 4 cups blueberries, sliced in half
- 4 tablespoons honey
- 2 tablespoons almonds, chopped

Method:

1. Fill the bowls with yogurt.
2. Add the fruits on top.
3. Drizzle with the honey and top with the chopped almonds.
4. Chill in the refrigerator for 10 minutes before serving.

Nutritional Value:

- Calories 478
- Total Fat 5.8g
- Saturated Fat 2.7g
- Cholesterol 15mg
- Sodium 178mg
- Total Carbohydrate 91.3g
- Dietary Fiber 8.4g
- Total Sugars 77.4g
- Protein 17.7g
- Potassium 1201mg

Fruit Crisps

Preparation Time: 20 minutes

Cooking Time: 30 minutes

Servings: 2

Ingredients:

- 1 cup cherries, chopped
- 1 cup peaches, chopped
- 1 cup pineapple chunks
- 1 cup apricots, chopped
- 1 cup apricots, chopped
- ¼ cup maple syrup
- 3 tablespoons lemon juice
- 3 tablespoons cornstarch
- ½ cup rolled oats
- ¼ cup almond meal
- ¼ cup almonds, sliced
- 3 tablespoons coconut oil
- ½ teaspoon ground cinnamon
- Salt to taste

Method:

1. Preheat your oven to 350 degrees F.
2. In a bowl, mix all the chopped fruits, maple syrup, lemon juice and cornstarch.
3. Place the fruits on metal bowls.
4. Top with a mixture of the rolled oats, almond meal, almonds, coconut oil, ground cinnamon and salt.
5. Bake in the oven for 30 minutes.

Nutritional Value:

- Calories 596
- Total Fat 28.8g
- Saturated Fat 18.6g
- Cholesterol 0mg
- Sodium 92mg
- Total Carbohydrate 83.6g
- Dietary Fiber 7.9g
- Total Sugars 46.8g
- Protein 7.6g
- Potassium 716mg

Fruit Cocktail with Oats

Preparation Time: 10 minutes

Cooking Time: 20 minutes

Serving: 1

Ingredients:

- 2 cups cooked oats
- 1 cup pineapple chunks
- 1 cup strawberry, sliced
- 1 cup blackberry, sliced
- 1 cup mango, cubed
- 1 tablespoon maple syrup
- 1 tablespoon almonds, chopped
- 1 tablespoon walnuts, chopped

Method:

1. Fill the bowl with cooked oats.
2. Place the fruits on top.
3. Drizzle with the maple syrup.
4. Sprinkle with the walnuts and almonds.

Nutritional Value:

- Calories 491
- Total Fat 9.8g
- Saturated Fat 1.2g
- Cholesterol 0mg
- Sodium 8mg
- Total Carbohydrate 91.8g
- Dietary Fiber 12.8g
- Total Sugars 29.8g
- Protein 13.9g
- Potassium 698mg

Berry Bowl

Preparation Time: 10 minutes

Cooking Time: 0 minute

Servings: 1

Ingredients:

- 1 cup blueberries, sliced in half
- 1 cup blackberries, sliced in half
- 1 cup strawberries, sliced in half
- ¼ cup cream cheese
- ¼ chopped pecans

Method:

1. Arrange the berries in a bowl.
2. Top with the cream cheese and pecans.
3. Serve.

Nutritional Value:

- Calories 393
- Total Fat 21.9g
- Saturated Fat 12.8g
- Cholesterol 64mg
- Sodium 176mg
- Total Carbohydrate 47.5g
- Dietary Fiber 14g
- Total Sugars 28.6g
- Protein 8.5g
- Potassium 634mg

Summer Fruits

Preparation Time: 20 minutes
Cooking Time: 5 minutes
Servings: 4
Ingredients:

- ¼ cup brown sugar
- ¼ cup orange juice
- ¼ cup lemon juice
- ½ teaspoon orange zest
- ½ teaspoon lemon zest
- 1 teaspoon vanilla extract
- 1 cup pineapple chunks
- 1 cup strawberry, cubed
- 1 kiwi fruit, sliced
- 1 banana, sliced
- 2 oranges, sliced
- 1 cup grapes, sliced in half
- 1 tablespoon chopped walnuts
- 1 tablespoon sunflower seeds

Method:

1. In a bowl, dissolve the brown sugar in the orange and lemon juices.
2. Stir in the orange and lemon zest.
3. Transfer to a pot and bring to a boil.
4. Simmer for 5 minutes.
5. Remove from heat and add the vanilla.
6. Arrange the fruits in layers.
7. Pour the syrup on top.
8. Sprinkle the walnuts and seeds on top of the fruits.

Nutritional Value:

- Calories 155
- Total Fat 0.6 g
- Saturated Fat 0 g
- Cholesterol 0 mg
- Sodium 5 mg
- Total Carbohydrates 39 g
- Dietary Fiber 12 g
- Total Sugars 29 g
- Protein 1.8 g
- Potassium 451 mg

Banana with Chia Seeds

Preparation Time: 10 minutes

Cooking Time: 0 minute

Serving: 1

Ingredients:

- 1 cup almond milk
- 3 tablespoons chia seeds
- 5 drops vanilla extract
- 1 tablespoon honey
- 2 bananas, sliced
- 1 tablespoon almonds, sliced
- 1 teaspoon coconut, grated

Method:

1. Pour the almond milk and vanilla extract in the blender.
2. Add the chia seeds and blend.
3. Put the banana on the bowl.
4. Drizzle the honey and almond milk on top.
5. Sprinkle with the almonds and coconut.

Nutritional Value:

- Calories 502
- Total Fat 35.1g
- Saturated Fat 26.3g
- Cholesterol 0mg
- Sodium 22mg
- Total Carbohydrate 49g
- Dietary Fiber 11g
- Total Sugars 27.2g
- Protein 7.1g
- Potassium 826mg

Apple & Banana Bowl

Preparation Time: 10 minutes

Cooking Time: 0 minute

Servings: 1

Ingredients:

- 1 cup apple, cubed
- 3 cups banana, cubed
- 1 cup dark chocolate syrup
- 4 cups cooked rolled oats

Method:

1. Fill the bowl with oats.
2. Top with the apple and banana cubes.
3. Drizzle with the dark chocolate syrup.

Nutritional Value:

- Calories 492
- Total Fat 6g
- Saturated Fat 1.1g
- Cholesterol 0mg
- Sodium 20mg
- Total Carbohydrate 101g
- Dietary Fiber 13g
- Total Sugars 29.7g
- Protein 12.5g
- Potassium 801mg

Conclusion

Each chapter focuses on a different foundation for your Buddha Bowl, so it's easy to prepare a large batch of wholesome grains to mix and match your meals throughout the week. Whether you're just starting to heal your body with a plant-based diet or you're building the foundation of healthy eating, these vibrant, nutrient-rich recipes are sure to help you on your health journey. With this plant-based Buddha Bowls recipe, you can always find inspirational, nutritious food that tastes good and makes you feel your best.

Thank you for buying this book, now start your food journey!